THE MYTH OF RUSSIAN COLLAPSE

China's Rise and Russia's Hidden Threat

Prabal Jain

Riverwood Capital

Riverwood Capital®

CONTENTS

INTRODUCTION

Russia against Ukraine

In the heat of battle during the late June 2023 skirmish known as the Battle of Bak Mud, an event of colossal magnitude unfolded within the Russian territory, momentarily seizing the gaze of the global audience. The Wagner Group, a Russian government-backed private military firm boasting a force of nearly 50,000 mercenaries and led by Yevgeni Pergosian, unexpectedly ignited a full-blown armed insurrection against the Russian government. This explosive rebellion followed over a year of relentless combat on the Ukrainian frontlines, where the Wagner Group had been a formidable pawn in Russia's military strategy. However, the battle for the town of Bakman, which lasted several grueling months, saw the Wagner Group sustaining heavy casualties. Pergosian reported a staggering loss of 20,000 mercenaries during this combat, a revelation that fueled his outspoken criticism towards the ineffective strategies deployed by the Russian military leadership in Ukraine. His discontent was often aimed at key figures like Russian Defense Minister Sergey Shoigu and Russian Chief of General Staff Valerie Garasimov, whom he accused of incompetence. Pergosian bemoaned the inadequate ammunition supplies for his troops and the abrupt retreats by the Russian military from frontline areas without prior notification, which frequently left the Wagner Group's flanks vulnerable to Ukrainian counterattacks. The simmering discord between the professional Russian army and the mercenary Wagner Group reached a boiling point on the fateful night of 23rd June 2023. On this day, Pergosian, albeit with scant evidence, accused the Russian military of a catastrophic friendly-fire missile attack on his troops, claiming the lives of an additional 2,000 mercenaries, and thereby declared rebellion.

Why Russia's Biggest Threat is Actually China

Rewinding the hands of time to 1858, China, under the rule of the Qing Dynasty, was embroiled in a monumental crisis. The country was grappling with a devastating internal civil war, claiming tens of millions of lives, while concurrently engaging with British and French forces in the Second Opium War. Seizing the moment of Chinese vulnerability, the Russian Empire mobilized tens of thousands of troops to the then border, demanding the cession of a vast territory known as Outer Manchuria. The Qing Dynasty, reluctant to ignite a third warfront against the Russians, acquiesced under duress, culminating in a 1860 treaty that relinquished a landmass equivalent to modern-day Ukraine to Russia without a single shot being fired. This strategic acquisition heralded the birth of significant Russian cities like Khabarovsk, now the largest city in the entire Russian Far East, and Vladivostok, the principal Russian port on the Pacific Ocean and the contemporary headquarters of the Russian Pacific Fleet, inclusive of nuclear-armed submarines. The significance of Vladivostok to Russia's naval and submarine nuclear deterrent capabilities in the Pacific cannot be overstated. However, this territorial gain came at a grave cost to China, barring direct access to the Sea of Japan and confining its maritime reach to the East and South China Seas. This historic event birthed a legacy of discontent among many Chinese nationalists, who view the loss of Outer Manchuria as yet another in a string of unequal treaties with foreign powers. Among them was the founder of the People's Republic of China, Mao Zedong. The 1960s witnessed a significant souring of relations between China and the Soviet Union, a deterioration rooted deeply in their historic past.

As we delve deeper into the historic and contemporary dynamics between Russia, China, and the global stage, the following chapters will unravel the nuanced narrative shrouding Russia's perceived decline and China's rising influence. Unpacking the intricate geopolitical landscape will offer a vantage point into the unseen threats and the prevailing myths that shape the Russian and Chinese narrative.

CHAPTER 1: THE INSURRECTION

A Prelude to Chaos

The undulating tensions between the Professional Russian army and the mercenary Wagner group reached a flashpoint on the night of 23rd June 2023. Yevgeni Pergosian, with tenuous evidence, alleged a malicious assault by the Russian military on his own forces, claiming the missile attacks resulted in the death of two thousand mercenaries. This accusation signaled the declaration of an armed rebellion by Pergosian and the Wagner group. The fiery demand was simple yet audacious: the surrender of Boshoku and Garasimov to face what Pergosian called 'his own justice'. He rallied approximately 20,000 of his mercenaries, withdrawing them from the Ukrainian front, and embarked on a brazen march back into Russian territory.

March Towards Moscow

Their first stop was the significant urban center of Rostov-on-Don, where they swiftly took control. This city, with a populace of around 1.2 million, became the initial stronghold for the Wagner group as the world tuned in, watching with bated breath the unfolding spectacle of an armed column marching unchallenged towards the Russian heartland.

With Rostov-on-Don under their belt, the Wagner group's procession thundered northward along the M4 Highway in a menacing cavalcade of tanks and trucks, seemingly unopposed.

Their audacious progress was marked by the capture of Voronezh, another significant Russian city with about 1.1 million residents. The march towards Moscow seemed almost inexorable, with each mile intensifying the palpable tension that had gripped the nation.

Putin's Denunciation and The Nation's Response

Amidst the escalating turmoil, Vladimir Putin took to the national airwaves, vehemently denouncing Pergosian and the Wagner group as treasonous traitors, vowing a ruthless retaliation. As the defiant convoy approached, hurried fortifications sprang up around Moscow. The capital braced itself, its skies intermittently pierced by the thud of military helicopters, attempting to halt the Wagner caravan but repeatedly being shot down. The eerie specter of a full-blown civil war loomed large over the Russian Federation.

However, as swiftly as the tempest had brewed, it subsided. Just a little over 24 hours post the declaration of rebellion, the situation deescalated, albeit leaving behind a trail of questions, fears, and a stark reminder of the fragility of order. The world had witnessed the audacity of a private military faction challenging a sovereign government, exposing the veiled fault lines within Russia's military apparatus.

As this chapter elucidates the Wagner uprising and its ripple effects, the subsequent chapters will delve deeper into the unfolding geopolitical intricacies, further examining Russia's internal and external threats, and the shadows cast by these events on Russia's global standing.

The Quick End to a Rebellion

The rebellion led by Yevgeni Pergosian and the Wagner group was looking like a big threat. But then, things changed quickly. Just 24 hours after it started, the rebellion stopped. This happened because of Alexander Lukashenko, the leader of Belarus, who is also a friend to the Kremlin. He talked with the groups and helped make a deal.

Because of Lukashenko's help, the Wagner group decided to put down their weapons. They left the cities of Voronezh and Rostov-on-Don that they had taken over. The charges against Pergosian and his group were dropped, and they went to Belarus, where they were safe. Though this rebellion was short, it did cause some harm - some soldiers and mercenaries were killed or hurt, and a few vehicles were destroyed.

This rebellion made people remember another tough time in 1993. Back then, President Boris Yeltsin had a big fight with the Russian Parliament. It ended with a violent attack on the House of the Soviets in Moscow, where many people were hurt or killed. Both times, in 1993 and now in 2023, it looked like Russia might have a civil war, but luckily, it didn't happen.

After the rebellion, many people talked and wrote about it. They said this rebellion showed that there would be more trouble in Russia in the future. Some said the problems in Ukraine might make things worse in Russia, just like past wars did. They compared it to how wars led to big changes in Russia before. But saying this misses the big picture of how Russia works today, which is something we will look at more in the next chapters.

As we move on, we will dig deeper into what's going on in Russia and how it deals with challenges both inside and outside the country.

CHAPTER 2: PREDICTING THE FALL

Putin's Enduring Reign

Many are quick to say that troubles in Russia, like the costly war in Ukraine, will lead to the end of the Russian Federation, much like past wars ended old Russian empires. They point to how the war in Afghanistan ended the Soviet Union, and World War One ended the tsarist Russian Empire. But, it's important to understand that predictions about the fall of Russian leaders, especially Vladimir Putin, have been made for a very long time.

Ever since Putin came to power, there have been many predictions about his fall. For example, when Ukraine fought back successfully in 2022 and took back over 13,000 square kilometers of land, many said Putin's end was near. There have also been endless talks about Putin's health, with some saying he might die any moment. When Russia invaded Ukraine in February 2022, and many people in Russia protested against the war, articles were written saying Putin was finished.

Even before that, during the COVID-19 pandemic, Russia struggled, and many people died. Some say between 400,000 to 820,000 Russians died. This was a big loss, and many thought it would lead to the end of Putin's rule.

There were other times too when people thought Putin would fall. When Volodymyr Zelensky became the president of Ukraine in 2019, or when Russia made unpopular changes to pension ages in 2018, or when Alexei Navalny became popular in Russia, many said these were signs of Putin's coming fall. Even back in 2014, when Russia took Crimea from Ukraine and the west put financial punishments on Russia, many said Putin's time was ending.

A Streak of Predicted Downfalls

The path of Vladimir Putin's reign has seen numerous predicaments, each sparking speculations about his political demise. The annexation of Crimea from Ukraine, the war in Donbas, and the Western financial sanctions post-2014 were seen as harbingers of Putin's fall. Even earlier, the anti-government protests of 2011 and 2012, Russia's foray into Georgia, the 2009 financial crisis, and the plunge in global oil prices were all tagged as the beginning of Putin's end. Going further back, the government's mishandling of terror attacks in 2004 and 2002, during the Beslan school siege and the Moscow theater hostage crisis, were deemed fatal for Putin's regime.

Despite the almost cyclical predictions of his political end, Putin's tenure has stood resilient through the storms. Ever since ascending to power in 2000, the Russian leader has faced a barrage of domestic and international challenges. Yet, as of 2023, he continues to firmly grip the reins of power, belying the prognostications of his downfall that have spanned over 23 years.

As recently as July 2023, an independent poll by the Levada Center showcased a robust approval rating of 82 percent for Putin. This level of public endorsement not only underscores the domestic support for Putin but also places him in a favorable light compared to many global leaders. For instance, the approval ratings of Joe Biden, Justin Trudeau, Rishi Sunak, Emmanuel Macron, and Fumio Kishida all trail significantly behind Putin's. Interestingly, only Volodymyr Zelensky of Ukraine surpasses Putin with a staggering 91 percent approval.

The resilience of Putin's regime is further mirrored in the manner in which domestic opposition has been handled. The anti-war protests that erupted in early 2022 faced a stringent crackdown, with close to 20,000 Russians arrested and detained. The repression drove hundreds of thousands to flee the country. Alexei Navalny, who is often viewed as the face of opposition to Putin in the West, also encountered the hard hand of the Kremlin.

Despite a tumultuous global stage and internal adversities, Putin's regime remains steadfast. The chapters ahead will delve into the mechanisms that fortify Putin's position and the interplay of domestic and international dynamics that contribute to the enduring nature of his reign.

CHAPTER 3: RESILIENCE AMID TURMOIL

Russia's Unwavering Stance

In early 2022, Russia witnessed a wave of anti-war protests that were swiftly and sternly dealt with. Around 20,000 Russians found themselves arrested and detained by authorities, while hundreds of thousands chose to flee the country to escape the repression. Among those targeted was Alexei Navalny, a figure often portrayed as the face of Russian opposition to Putin in the West. Navalny was sentenced to 30 years in a Siberian penal colony on charges of alleged fraud and extremism, with additional terrorism charges looming. At 47 years old, the likelihood of Navalny spending the rest of his life behind bars seems high, unless the popular Putin-led regime comes to an end.

Western Sanctions: A Failed Deterrent?

Despite occupying about a fifth of Ukraine's internationally recognized territory, a landmass comparable to the size of Austria, Russia's economy and society appeared to remain largely unaffected by the war. This stability came as a surprise to many, especially considering the decision-making that ensued post the invasion.

Western powers, including the US, EU, and UK, united in imposing an unprecedented amount of financial sanctions on Russia, aiming to trigger a financial collapse. Officials within the Biden

Administration had projected these sanctions, termed the most consequential in world history, to slash Russia's economy by as much as 50 percent. Contrary to these Western anticipations of a financial catastrophe for Moscow, the Russian economy only contracted by a modest 2.1 percent by the end of 2022. This contraction was lower than what Russia experienced during the COVID-19 pandemic, the 2009 global financial crisis, or the economic transition tumult of the 1990s.

Bouncing Back: Economic Growth Post-2022

Astonishingly, the International Monetary Fund (IMF) now forecasts a rebound for the Russian economy. It's expected to grow by as much as 1.5 percent in 2023, with the growth trend predicted to continue into 2024. This recovery effectively undoes the economic shrinkage experienced earlier, displaying a level of economic resilience that defied many predictions.

Simultaneously, the leisure pursuits of Russian civilians appear undeterred. An estimated seven million Russian tourists are projected to visit Turkey in the current year alone, which is nearly five percent of Russia's total population. Additionally, millions are flocking to other popular destinations like Egypt, the UAE, the Maldives, and Thailand. Surprisingly, many of these travelers are being transported on government-seized Boeing and Airbus aircraft operated by Russian-owned airlines.

The existing scenario sharply contrasts with the West's earlier portrayal of an impending financial Armageddon for Russia. This narrative was spun around a year and a half ago, assuming it to be an inevitable consequence of Western sanctions.

A Harsher Reality for Ukraine

On the flip side, Ukraine's economy has been severely battered, losing a fifth of its territory to a hostile invasion, enduring mass exodus of its citizens, and suffering extensive infrastructure damage from relentless missile, drone, and rocket attacks. Additionally, a stifling Russian naval blockade has severely hampered its exports and imports. Consequently, Ukraine's economy plummeted by an estimated 29.1 percent by the end of 2022, in stark contrast to Russia's minor 2.1 percent contraction.

The financial face-off between the Western world and Russia seems to be morphing into a stalemate, mirroring the military deadlock on the Ukrainian frontlines. The Ukrainian counter-offensive is finding it tough to penetrate Russian defenses. To comprehend how Russia, under Putin's leadership, has managed to withstand the enormous pressures of Western sanctions, the catastrophic military casualties in Ukraine, and still maintain a semblance of normalcy domestically requires an exploration into the source of Russia's modern power.

The unfolding dynamics present a multi-faceted picture of resilience, defiance, and unexpected economic recovery on Russia's part amid ongoing geopolitical tensions. The subsequent chapters will delve deeper into the heart of Russia's modern power, the geopolitical chessboard, and how this protracted conflict is shaping the broader region.

CHAPTER 4: THE ENERGY SHIFT

Unintended Consequences and Strategic Realignments

Russia's gargantuan landmass is not just a geographical marvel but a treasure trove of critical resources and raw materials crucial for modern developing civilizations globally. The lands of Russia host about a quarter of the world's discovered reserves of natural gas, the largest held by any single country. Besides, Russia ranks second in coal reserves and sixth in oil reserves. Despite its relative small population and economy compared to neighboring giants like China, Japan, and Germany, Russia's bounty of resources positions it as a significant player on the global stage.

Historically, Russia has been the world's largest exporter of natural gas and the second-largest exporter of oil, trailing slightly behind Saudi Arabia. These massive exports have not only funneled vast revenues into the Russian state but also handed it immense leverage over nations dependent on its energy supplies. Just before the invasion of Ukraine in January 2022, the oil and gas sector accounted for a staggering 45 percent of the government's annual budget and 60 percent of all state exports. This stark dependency enshrines Russia as Europe's only true petrostate, akin to Saudi Arabia or Iran in their reliance on resource exports for governmental sustenance.

The symbiotic relationship between Russia and Western

Europe has been shaped by geographical proximity and mutual dependencies. Wealthy yet energy-resource-poor Western European countries have historically relied on Russia's energy exports. This interdependency has fostered a relationship bound by geography and a mutual craving for what the other possesses.

The Tug of Economic Dependencies: The Aftermath of Invasion

The economic dance between Russia and Western Europe was choreographed by a simple principle: Western Europe had wealth but lacked energy resources, while Russia had abundant oil and gas reserves but needed financial stability. This symbiosis was further facilitated by a network of overland pipelines, meticulously constructed over decades, ensuring a steady flow of energy from Russia to Europe at costs lower than alternative sources.

In 2021, about half of Russia's oil exports found their way to Europe, satisfying 45 percent of the entire European Union's natural gas needs. This trade funneled approximately $148 billion into Russia's coffers, reflecting a mutually beneficial relationship defined by geographical and economic pragmatism. However, the harmony was disrupted when Russian troops marched into Ukraine in early 2022. The Western World retaliated by announcing an end to energy trade with Russia. By the close of 2022, Russian energy exports to the EU, UK, and US were either obliterated or drastically curtailed, aiming to choke off financial resources needed for Russia's military endeavors in Ukraine.

The US acted swiftly, halting its relatively modest imports of oil and gas from Russia almost immediately post-invasion. The European Union, being traditionally Moscow's largest energy market, faced a more complex adjustment process. Nevertheless, by the end of 2022, the EU had virtually halted all seaborne

Russian oil imports and slashed Russia's share in its natural gas imports from around 45 percent pre-invasion to below 10 percent at the dawn of 2023.

To mitigate the sudden void of Russian oil and gas, the European Union turned to alternative sources. New energy channels were established, with additional piped gas flowing in from Norway, Algeria, and Azerbaijan. This was coupled with a drastic ramp-up in liquified natural gas (LNG) imports, endeavoring to stabilize the European energy landscape that had been violently shaken.

Adapting to the Energy Void: Europe's Quest for Alternatives

As the energy lifeline from Russia snapped, Europe scurried to fill the enormous gap in oil and gas supply. The solution emerged from diversified sources, with additional piped gas coming from Norway, Algeria, and Azerbaijan, supplemented by a significant surge in seabound LNG imports from Qatar and the United States. By the end of 2023, the latter had replaced Russia as Europe's largest single natural gas provider. The transition reflected Europe's resilience and the global energy market's dynamic nature in adapting to abrupt geopolitical shifts.

The Nord Stream Setback: Symbolizing the Severed Energy Ties

The disengagement between Russia and Europe culminated dramatically with the mysterious bombings of the twin Nord Stream pipelines beneath the Baltic Sea in late 2022. This assault rendered the $20 billion project, which once stood as a monument to Russia-Europe energy cooperation, utterly dysfunctional. The bombings resonated beyond the immediate loss, symbolizing the dramatic end of a longstanding energy-for-money relationship.

As the Western world tightened the economic noose around Russia to choke off its war machine in Ukraine, a complex dilemma unfolded. The West understood that overly stringent sanctions could backfire. If Russia's energy exports were entirely blocked, the resulting void would equate to an 11% cut in the global oil production, potentially triggering a catastrophic global supply shock. This scenario threatened to send oil prices soaring to new heights, inflicting worsened inflation worldwide, as businesses would pass on the higher energy costs to consumers.

The delicate balance needed to ensure Russia's continued oil exports without financially empowering its war endeavors required nuanced strategies. The objective was clear: maintain a steady global oil supply while simultaneously isolating Russia to curb its military aggression in Ukraine.

The Price Cap Sanction: A Novel Strategy to Curb Russian Aggression

Amidst the tensions between Russia and the Western World, a unique strategy arose from the G7 Nations to maintain global oil supply stability while simultaneously stifling Russia's war revenues. This chapter delves into the 'Price Cap Sanction' and its impact on the global oil market and Russian oil revenues.

The G7 Nations, encompassing the United States, Canada, the European Union, United Kingdom, Japan, plus Australia, orchestrated a 'Price Cap Sanction' on Russian oil. This sanction permits maritime service companies within these nations to continue aiding the transportation of Russian oil and petroleum products globally, albeit under a stringent price cap of sixty dollars a barrel. This price cap is notably below the global benchmark price, which hovered between 70 and 82 dollars per barrel throughout 2023.

The Price Cap Sanction leverages the dominant position of the G7 countries plus Australia in the maritime insurance and services sector, which accounts for about 90% of the global market.

Maritime activities worldwide necessitate legitimate insurance—a service primarily provided by companies operating within these nations. The sanction, therefore, forces Russia to adhere to the price cap if it wishes to retain access to these crucial maritime services, thereby reducing the revenues it can generate from oil exports.

The sanction aims to hit Russia where it hurts the most—its oil revenues—without disrupting the global oil supply. By enforcing a price cap, the G7 Nations have created a scenario where Russia must sell its oil at lower prices to maintain its export volumes. The lower price not only diminishes Russia's war finances but also provides other nations with a bargaining chip to negotiate lower prices, capitalizing on Russia's constrained selling conditions.

CHAPTER 5: REDIRECTING THE FLOW

*Russia's Pivot to Eastern
and African Markets*

Amidst the Western sanctions, Russia sought new horizons for its oil and gas exports, redirecting its focus towards Asia and Africa. This chapter analyzes the shift in trade dynamics and its economic implications for Russia and the global energy market. By mid-2023, the Price Cap Sanction had visibly impacted Russia's oil revenue. From January to June 2023, Russia's earnings from oil sales to foreign markets plummeted to about $37.4 billion, less than half of what it had accrued during the first half of 2022. This demonstrated the effectiveness of the sanction in crippling Russia's revenue streams while maintaining a steady global oil supply.

With diminishing access to European and North American markets and constrained by the price cap in other markets, Russia was propelled to reroute its oil and gas exports predominantly to Asian and African countries. Pre-invasion, the geographical proximity made Europe a more economical destination for Russian energy exports, while the Persian Gulf supplied the bulk of oil to Asia and Africa. Post-invasion, the equation changed.

Historically, shipping Russian oil to far-flung Asian and African markets wasn't as economically sensible due to higher transportation costs compared to Middle Eastern oil. However, the price cap sanction, which forced Russia to sell its oil at significantly lower prices, made Russian oil a more attractive option despite the relatively higher shipping costs. The substantial discount on Russian oil overshadowed the logistical costs, making it an attractive option for countries in these regions.

The Shifting Sands of Oil Diplomacy

The reverberations of the Ukraine conflict continue to reshape the global energy market dynamics. Two emerging trends are the redirection of Russian oil exports and the ensuing competition between Russia and Saudi Arabia in Asian markets, particularly in India and China. This chapter delves into these developments and their broader implications.

The Indian Transition

The transformation in India's oil import landscape is remarkable. Before the invasion, Russian oil constituted an insignificant share of India's oil imports. However, by late 2023, Russian oil accounts for a massive 40% of India's oil imports. This transition has consequently impacted Saudi Arabia, whose market share in India's oil imports has dwindled from 20% pre-invasion to about 13%.

The Sino-Russian-Saudi Oil Triangle

China, possessing the world's largest energy market, has become a battleground for oil export supremacy between Russia and Saudi Arabia. The price advantage of Russian oil has enticed China to double its imports from Russia from the onset of the invasion to May 2023. The dynamics have now shifted, with Russia and Saudi Arabia almost neck-and-neck in terms of market share in China's oil imports, and projections indicate Russia might overtake Saudi Arabia by the year-end.

As Russia gains market share in Asia, Saudi Arabia faces a revenue shortfall, threatening its ambitious Vision 2030 reforms. To mitigate revenue losses stemming from reduced market share and the price cap on Russian oil, Russia and Saudi Arabia have orchestrated a joint cut in their oil production throughout 2023. This move aims to tighten global oil supply, pushing up prices to increase their revenues. By September 2023, both countries are expected to curtail their production to around 9 million barrels of oil per day, a significant reduction from their 2022 levels.

In a bid to counter the inflationary pressures exacerbated by the Saudi-Russian production cut, the United States plans to ramp up its oil production to a record 12.6 million barrels per day in 2023. This strategic move is designed to inject more oil into the global market, aiming to stabilize or lower the global oil prices, and in turn, alleviate inflationary pressures.

The Global Oil Chessboard

The global oil market is at the center of a geopolitical tug-of-war, featuring key players with contrasting objectives. This chapter explores the unfolding "oil war" between the US and Europe on one side, and Russia and Saudi Arabia on the other, and the strategies they are employing to safeguard their interests amid the ongoing crises.

The heart of the matter is the diverging interests over oil prices. The US and Europe aim for lower prices to curb inflation and to hamstring Russia's war efforts in Ukraine. Conversely, Russia seeks higher prices to fund its military campaign and stabilize its economy, while Saudi Arabia desires additional revenue to propel its extensive economic and societal reforms.

Despite being edged out of traditional markets, Russia finds solace in neutral countries like China, India, and Turkey, maintaining a steady flow of oil and gas sales. The European Union, albeit at a reduced volume, continues to purchase Russian energy resources, albeit the trajectory is downwards as alternative supplies are sought.

Tactical Alliance: Russia and Saudi Arabia

Russia and Saudi Arabia have tactically synchronized their oil supply strategies to bolster global oil prices. This cooperation has yielded a slow but steady rise in prices, allowing Russia to inch past the price cap imposed by the G7 plus Australia coalition, with trading prices of Russian oil touching seventy dollars per barrel by mid-2023.

The modest triumph in breaching the price cap inspires Russia to anticipate higher oil revenues in the latter half of 2023. This optimism is mirrored in Russia's bold move to augment its defense spending in August 2023, allocating over five percent of its GDP, which propels its military budget past the 100 billion dollars mark, ranking third globally behind China and the United States. The choreography of oil diplomacy unveils a complex, high-stakes game where nations tactically navigate to protect their interests. The unfolding events underscore the intertwined nature of energy markets with geopolitical objectives and economic stability. As the oil war simmers, the reverberations are felt far beyond the principal actors, hinting at a continually evolving global oil landscape with potential long-term ramifications.

CHAPTER 6: THE COMPLEX WEB OF SANCTIONS

Military Stalemate, and Economic Resilience

Amid the ongoing conflict, Russia and Ukraine are channeling significant resources into their military apparatus. This military-centric spending is not only reshaping their economies but also impacting the livelihoods of their citizens. This chapter delves into this military Keynesianism phenomenon and its implications on the war-torn region. Russia's defense budget soared to over $100 billion in 2023, marking a historical peak since the Soviet era. This ramp-up, accounting for more than five percent of its GDP, signifies a transition towards a wartime economy. On the flip side, Ukraine's defense spending escalated to an astounding 18.3% of its GDP, now the third highest globally, only trailing the militaristic regimes of North Korea and Eritrea.

The international community's support has been pivotal for Ukraine, with over $100 billion in military aid, $60 billion of which came from the US. This substantial aid levels the financial playing field, enabling Ukraine to somewhat match Russia's military spending despite its smaller economic and industrial base.

The war effort is fueling industrial activity in Russia, with substantial resources directed towards the manufacture of military goods ranging from uniforms to sophisticated weaponry.

This synergy between military spending and industrial output, termed as military Keynesianism, is momentarily boosting Russia's economy while benefiting the military-industrial complex.

In a parallel stride, the Russian government is amplifying social spending programs to uplift pensions, salaries, and subsidized housing facilities. The war has also become a source of higher income for soldiers and significant compensation for the families of the fallen, momentarily improving the financial circumstances for a portion of the population.

A Balancing Act: Deficit Spending and Economic Resilience

Russia's current economic model is a meticulous balancing act. Despite the slash in oil and gas revenues, which were the lifeblood of its economy, Russia has ramped up military and social spending. This chapter explores the mechanisms behind Russia's economic resilience and the lurking challenges that could potentially destabilize its financial equilibrium.

The plummet in oil and gas revenues left a significant dent in Russia's financial structure. Yet, the nation opts for deficit spending to sustain military operations and bolster social spending. As of May 2023, the projected budget deficit stood at around $41 billion. However, with rising oil prices, newer estimates suggest a deficit of $28 billion by year-end. This deficit spending is underpinned by the hope of recovering oil and gas revenues, which, if realized, could gradually offset the deficit.

Debt Levels: A Silver Lining

One of Russia's economic strongholds is its relatively low national debt, which as of July 2023, totals $250.8 billion, equating to merely 15% of its annual GDP. This positions Russia with the lowest debt amongst the top 20 global economies, granting it a substantial leeway to manage its deficit. Theoretically, at the current deficit levels, Russia could sustain this spending model for decades before nearing the debt proportions of nations like the United States.

Despite the seemingly sturdy economic facade, there are burgeoning challenges. A prominent concern is Russia's tight labor market and the chronic worker shortage. The population was already on a decline pre-invasion, and the situation has further exacerbated with the ongoing military engagement. The labor shortage could potentially stymie industrial output and economic growth in the longer run.

The dwindling population and the resultant labor shortages pose a significant challenge. Russia's ability to maintain its industrial and military operations hinges on a robust workforce. However, with a declining population, fulfilling these labor requirements becomes an uphill task. This, in the long run, could potentially thwart Russia's economic and military ambitions.

The Labor Conundrum and Economic Resilience Amid Sanctions

The Russian economy showcases a facade of stability amid escalating geopolitical tensions. However, beneath this semblance of resilience lies a brewing labor crisis and a complex web of international trade dynamics. This chapter delves into the labor shortage exacerbated by military mobilization and explores how Russia navigates economic sanctions through alternative trade channels.

The labor market in Russia is grappling with a chronic shortage of workers, a problem rooted in the nation's declining population.

The mobilization of 300,000 additional men, primarily from the blue-collar sector, for the Ukrainian front in September 2022 further strained the labor force. The exodus of hundreds of thousands post-invasion has accentuated the crisis. The labor shortage not only hampers industrial output but also poses a hurdle for further military mobilization, which could potentially trigger economic and political instability.

Western sanctions have curtailed the influx of migrant workers, as their ability to remit earnings back home is restricted. This exacerbates the labor shortage, as Russia has traditionally relied on migrant labor to fill gaps in its workforce. The scenario presents a Catch-22 situation: mobilizing additional manpower for the war could intensify the labor crisis, adversely impacting the economy, while the sanctions impede the alternative of replenishing the labor force with migrant workers.

Navigating the Sanctions: The Eurasian Economic Union and Beyond

Despite the crippling sanctions, Russia has found a workaround through the Eurasian Economic Union (EAEU), which facilitates free trade among its member states. While Russia and Belarus face stringent western financial sanctions, fellow EAEU members Kazakhstan, Kyrgyzstan, and Armenia do not. This arrangement enables a discreet conduit for Russia to access essential goods from the West, through these nations.

Moreover, Chinese and Turkish firms have emerged as alternative channels for Russia to procure vital resources, including advanced semiconductors and computer chips, essential for sustaining its military operations in Ukraine.

Sanctions and Economic Adaptability

Despite the Western sanctions, Russia's economy displays remarkable adaptability. A case in point is the continued supply of crucial military components like advanced chips and lasers for its operations in Ukraine. Additionally, the seized Boeing and Airbus aircraft, operated by Russian-owned airlines, continue to ferry Russian tourists worldwide. This operational continuity, even under sanctions, is facilitated by maintenance and repair services available in neutral countries like Turkey, Egypt, and the United Arab Emirates.

The sanctions' effectiveness is further diluted as Russia leverages its relationships with neutral or friendly nations. The existing sanctions framework faces challenges in extending compliance ultimatums without alienating key neutral countries, demonstrating the complex geopolitical landscape that underpins the economic war.

The military front in Ukraine reflects a stalemate, mirroring the economic standoff. Ukraine's ambition to reclaim lost territories, including Crimea, faces a formidable obstacle in the heavily fortified frontlines stretching over a thousand kilometers. The extensive defense structures, trenches, and notably, the prolific planting of landmines by both Russian and Ukrainian forces, have created an almost insurmountable barrier. The landmine situation, with estimates suggesting millions scattered across an area the size of Florida, underscores the daunting challenge ahead.

Unfolding Geopolitical Alliances

The evolving conflict unveils a kaleidoscope of geopolitical alignments. The stalemate in the energy and economic war between the West and Russia reflects a broader global impasse. While the sanctions aim to isolate Russia economically, its geographical size, resource abundance, and alliances with neutral or friendly countries undermine this objective.

Russia's ability to sustain its economy and military operations despite sanctions has, in turn, maintained President Putin's popularity, further entrenching the stalemate both economically and on the battlefield.

The Grind of Warfare and a Gleam of Hope

The conflict between Russia and Ukraine has left the land marred with the remnants of war, notably, the extensive landmines scattered across the Ukrainian soil. This chapter delves into the challenges faced by Ukraine in navigating through a heavily fortified defensive line, the ongoing struggle for reclaiming lost territories, and the external support that provides a glimmer of hope amid a grim demographic scenario.

The landmine issue in Ukraine is not just a military challenge but a humanitarian crisis in waiting. With estimates of millions of landmines planted across an area comparable to Florida, the cleanup task post-conflict would require a monumental effort spanning generations and necessitating tens of billions of dollars. The landmine contamination ranks Ukraine among the most heavily affected countries globally, setting a daunting stage for any military advancement.

Military Stalemate: The Air and Ground Dilemma

The conventional military strategy to overcome heavily fortified defenses involves employing a substantial amount of airstrikes to create a breach for ground forces. However, Ukraine faces a significant handicap with a deficient Air Force, rendering this strategy unviable. The alternative is a ground assault on the well-prepared defenses, a tactic fraught with danger, slow progression, and likely heavy casualties. The formidable Russian defenses, coupled with extensive minefields, present a quagmire for the Ukrainian counter-offensive efforts, underlining the slow and grinding nature of this conflict.

Despite the military and demographic challenges, Ukraine's resilience is bolstered by substantial military aid from Western democracies. The inflow of tens of billions of dollars in military aid and equipment is a lifeline for Ukraine, offsetting the military imbalance to some extent. This external support is crucial for Ukraine to stand a chance against a more potent Russian force and to harbor hopes of reclaiming lost territories.

Post the Soviet Union collapse, Ukraine experienced a demographic decline, a trend that has exacerbated with the ongoing conflict. The demographic profile of Ukraine, compared unfavorably even to Russia's, underscores a long-term concern that extends beyond the immediate military challenges. The stark population decline since the Soviet era is a bleak backdrop against which the battle for reclaiming territories is being fought.

The Tug of War – A Deep Dive into Demographics and Manpower

The ongoing conflict between Ukraine and Russia unfolds against a backdrop of stark demographic contrasts and military capabilities. This chapter explores the demographic narratives of both nations, their military manpower, and the implications on the battlefield.

Post the disintegration of the Soviet Union, Ukraine's population has been on a downward trajectory. Peaking at about 52.4 million in 1993, the population saw a reduction of more than 10 million by 2021, just before the invasion. The invasion further exacerbated this decline, with millions fleeing the country. This massive population drop, now standing at a little over 36 million, significantly impacts Ukraine's military manpower, presenting a grim picture of the country's capacity to withstand prolonged conflict.

Russia's Demographic Steadiness

In contrast, Russia has maintained a relatively steady population, with the current figure of around 145 million only slightly down from its peak in 1992. The demographic steadiness provides Russia with a substantially larger pool of military-aged men, thereby establishing a decisive manpower advantage on the battlefield.

The available manpower for military service outlines a significant disparity between the two nations. While Russia boasts around 47 million men fit for military service, Ukraine may only have around 15 million. This disparity extends to the number of men reaching military age annually, further widening the gap in military recruitment potential.

The demographic and manpower disparities manifest conspicuously on the battlefield. With a significantly larger troop deployment, Russia has managed to maintain a robust front line in Ukraine. The Ukrainian forces, though valiant, find themselves in a challenging position to overcome the Russian defenses due to a comparative lack of manpower. The disparity in troop numbers and the ability to replenish lost personnel could potentially influence the strategic decisions and the pace at which the conflict unfolds.

The Financial Frontline – Examining Ukraine's Fiscal Fortitude

The financial dynamics of the ongoing conflict between Ukraine and Russia are as complex as the military engagements on the ground. This chapter delves into Ukraine's fiscal response to the invasion, exploring the extraordinary rise in defense spending and its implications on the nation's economy and international relations.

In the face of existential threat post-invasion, Ukraine ramped up its defense spending to an unprecedented $44 billion in 2022, reflecting a more than sevenfold increase from the previous year. Despite a 30% contraction in the nation's GDP due to the conflict, this surge in defense spending catapulted Ukraine into a total war-style economy, dedicating over 27% of its GDP to defense — the highest global percentage as of 2023.

A comparative look at Ukraine's historical budgets unveils the enormity of this financial pivot. The total government budget hovered around $18.7 billion annually between 1989 and 2021, peaking at $36.1 billion in 2021 in the wake of the COVID-19 pandemic. However, the defense spending alone in 2022 and 2023 surpasses the entire national budget of 2021, underlining the fiscal realignment Ukraine has undergone to sustain its resistance.

The financial exigencies of war, coupled with the loss in exports and lack of substantial natural resource revenues like Russia, have pushed Ukraine into a historic deficit, projected at about $40 billion for 2023. This deficit underscores the economic precariousness but also the indomitable resolve of Ukraine in its fight for sovereignty.

The fiscal shortfall is significantly cushioned by robust financial support from Ukraine's allies, particularly the United States, Europe, and the IMF. Over $100 billion in direct military aid and assistance has flowed into Ukraine since the invasion commenced, with $60 billion emanating from the United States alone. This level of support, even when adjusted for inflation, surpasses the aid extended to the Mujahideen during the 1980s Soviet conflict, indicating a profound international commitment to Ukraine's cause.

Ukraine's fiscal narrative is emblematic of a nation rallying its resources and garnering substantial international support to withstand an overpowering adversary. The financial frontline, though strained, holds a pivotal position in Ukraine's overarching strategy for survival and eventual triumph. As the fiscal commitments deepen, the international alliances' steadfastness will likely continue to be a critical factor in the unfolding narrative of Ukraine's struggle for independence.

The Fiscal Cliff - Ukraine's Economic Precipice

The ongoing war has led Ukraine to a fiscal cliff, with unprecedented military spending and foreign aid keeping it from plummeting. However, the horizon post-war presents a dire picture, teetering on unsustainable debt levels and an enormous rebuilding cost. This chapter delves into the economic challenges and uncertainties looming over Ukraine.

Ukraine's shift to a total war economy, dedicating over a quarter of its GDP to military spending, reflects a desperate measure in desperate times. Additionally, the $100 billion in military aid has momentarily balanced the fiscal scales against Russia. However, the sustainability of this financial model is in serious doubt, especially with uncertainties surrounding continued foreign support.

The war's cataclysmic impact on Ukraine's infrastructure is another ticking fiscal time bomb. The constant onslaught has left behind a trail of destruction, with the World Bank estimating a staggering $350 billion needed for a complete rebuild - a sum that doubles the nation's current GDP. This doesn't even factor in the cost of demining the land and dealing with unexploded ordnances, a monumental task in itself.

The fiscal exigencies have driven Ukraine's national debt through the roof, standing at around $162 billion as of mid to late 2023, mirroring the nation's entire annual GDP. The war, though fought valiantly, is pushing Ukraine into a debt quagmire that threatens to engulf its economy in a long-term crisis.

Even a victorious outcome in the war leaves Ukraine facing a Herculean task of rebuilding, a task it cannot afford. With a debt to GDP ratio threatening to soar to 320%, Ukraine is on a fast track to becoming the most heavily indebted country globally. This precarious fiscal position almost guarantees a default unless substantial external financial support is rendered for reconstruction.

The fiscal cliff Ukraine finds itself on is steep and slippery. The monumental task of rebuilding post-war and servicing an exploding national debt requires a robust and sustained international financial commitment. Whether through war reparations from Russia or continued aid from the West, Ukraine's economic survival and stability post-conflict hinge on external financial support. The unfolding scenario underscores the profound and lasting economic scars of war, which extend far beyond the battlefield.

CHAPTER 7: THE RUSSIAN RESILIENCE AND UKRAINIAN RESOLVE

Ukraine stands at a precarious juncture, where the sustainability of financial aid, domestic capacity, and geopolitical support are in a delicate balance. The chapter explores the country's race against time and resources in confronting well-entrenched Russian defenses, while navigating the choppy waters of international support and internal capacities.

The umbilical cord of foreign aid, amounting to over $160 billion, has been keeping Ukraine's fight alive. This massive inflow, led by the United States, has acted as a counterbalance to Russia's superior manpower and industrial strength. However, the continuity of this lifeline is far from certain, with the tides of political opinion and fiscal considerations in donor countries threatening to alter the course of support.

The war is more than a battlefield confrontation for Ukraine; it's a pressure cooker situation where every delay amplifies the financial strain and stretches the fragile thread of international aid. The dire need to break through Russian defenses is as much about military victory as it is about showcasing the efficacy and viability of Ukrainian resistance to keep the tap of foreign aid flowing.

On the domestic front, the clock is ticking against Ukraine. The mounting debt, ballooning budget deficit, and a war-ravaged economy paint a grim picture. The war's drain on the already scarce resources is a ticking time bomb, threatening to implode the economy if the war drags on without significant breakthroughs or a resumption of normalcy.

As the 2024 U.S. presidential election looms, the question of financial support to Ukraine is becoming a hot potato. A CNN poll revealing a majority of Americans opposing further aid to Ukraine reflects a changing mood, potentially altering the calculus of support. The voices against aid are growing louder, and Ukraine's situation is fast becoming a pawn in a larger political game.

The race against time and resources for Ukraine is a harrowing journey on a tightrope, with the abyss of financial ruin on one side and the phantom of military defeat on the other. The challenge for Ukraine is not merely about breaking through fortified defenses; it's about breaking free from a vicious cycle where military action, financial ruin, and dwindling international support are intertwined in a deadly dance. This situation underscores the cold reality of geopolitics and the intricate weave of military action, international support, and domestic capacity in determining the fate of nations embroiled in conflicts.

Russia's Historical Backbone

Russia's military strategy is deeply rooted in its historical experiences, where sustained losses in past conflicts led to significant political shifts. The ghosts of World War I and the Afghan War linger in the collective memory, shaping the nation's approach towards the conflict in Ukraine. However, a key distinction lies in the demographic and political fabric of the modern Russian Federation compared to its historical predecessors.

Russia appears to be playing a long game, drawing parallels to past U.S. engagements in Vietnam and Afghanistan, aiming for a war of attrition to drain Western support for Ukraine. The stalemate on the Ukrainian front, coupled with a focus shift to Asia, particularly China and Taiwan, may dilute the Western resolve, potentially leading to a reduction in financial aid to Ukraine. This strategic patience is a gamble on international attention and resources, reflecting a cold calculus of endurance.

On the flip side, Ukraine's situation is growing more precarious with each passing day. The pressure to penetrate well-entrenched Russian defenses is amplified by the looming risk of dwindling international support. The desperate need for a breakthrough is as much about military victory as it is about sustaining the financial lifeline from the West.

The toll of the conflict extends beyond the battlefield. Russia's estimated loss of 65,000 soldiers with another 150,000 wounded is a silent testimony to the human cost. The comparison of these figures to historical military losses underscores the severity of the ongoing conflict. Yet, the expected ripple of discontent within Russia remains muted, challenging the historical narrative of internal upheaval following military catastrophes.

The Evolution of Russian Stability Amidst Unrest

The discourse surrounding the stability of modern-day Russia often finds its roots in historical upheavals witnessed during significant military losses. Yet, the socio-political landscape has evolved, rendering old parallels less direct in illustrating Russia's present-day resilience or potential susceptibility to internal strife.

Historically, the vast and diverse ethnic composition within the Russian Empire and later the Soviet Union often fueled separatist movements, especially during times of national crises. However, contemporary Russia showcases a shift towards a more homogenous demographic makeup, with 81% of its population being ethnically Russian as per the 2021 census. This evolution underscores a more unified national identity, reducing the fissures for ethnic or nationalist-based separatist movements.

Modern-day Russia houses fewer regions where ethnic Russians are in the minority. Among these, only three areas - Dagestan, Chechnya, and Ingushetia, known for their historical tendencies towards separatism, present plausible flashpoints for localized unrest. The centralized power and high approval ratings for Putin, standing at 82%, exhibit a strong national backing, diminishing the likelihood of widespread separatist movements across the federation.

Russia's economy, buoyed by its rich natural resource base, especially oil, forms the bedrock of its financial stability. Nevertheless, a hypothetical sudden plummet in oil prices could strain the government's ability to maintain its budgetary commitments. The ongoing military engagement in Ukraine, coupled with potential economic strain, could test Russia's financial resilience.

The speculation of a civil war hinges on a series of adverse events, including an economic downturn and escalating military casualties in Ukraine. The combination of financial stress and heightened national grief could create internal discord. However, the strong nationalistic fervor and centralized political power provide a buffer against such speculations.

Bakmut Battle: An Inflection Point in Contemporary European History

Amidst the larger geopolitical canvas painted with economic, political, and military hues, lies the battle for Bakmut in Eastern Ukraine—a striking manifestation of escalating tensions and a harbinger of wider ramifications for Ukraine, Russia, and the broader Eastern European region.

The Russian involvement in Ukraine's affairs, accentuated by the ferocious battle for Bakmut, reflects a broader canvas of geopolitical struggle. This confrontation, reminiscent of the intense trench warfare witnessed during World War One, unveils a new yet brutal chapter in European military engagements since World War Two.

The brutal engagements around Bakmut have evoked comparisons with the Battle of Erdah from World War One. The trench warfare, a grim reminder of historical military stalemates, brings to the fore a dire reality that Europe hoped had been relegated to the annals of history. The parallel drawn here not only underscores the intensity of the confrontation but also the potential historical significance the outcome holds.

Russia's venture in Ukraine, exemplified by the battle for Bakmut, delineates the military and economic strains it's navigating. The conundrum of maintaining military engagement amidst an uncertain economic landscape, exacerbated by potential oil price fluctuations and sanctions, poses a critical challenge. The war's human and financial toll, juxtaposed against Russia's economic vulnerabilities, could strain its resources and potentially impact Putin's standing domestically.

The ongoing battle transcends the immediate military objectives, bearing implications for the geopolitical equilibrium in Eastern Europe. The support from Western nations to Ukraine, juxtaposed against Russia's military endeavors, renders Bakmut a focal point of broader geopolitical interests. Amidst these military confrontations, the Wagner Rebellion unfurled, albeit prematurely and under seemingly favorable circumstances for Putin. This rebellion, though quelled, hints at the underlying political tensions within Russia and the potential for internal discord under altered economic and military circumstances.

The Battle for Bakmut is more than a military engagement; it's a complex interplay of historical, geopolitical, and internal political dynamics. Its outcome could set a precedent, influencing the geopolitical trajectory of not only Ukraine and Russia but also the wider Eastern European region. The historical analogies evoke a grim reflection, while the unfolding realities offer a glimpse into the evolving narrative of modern-day geopolitical conflicts and the fragile equilibrium that hangs in the balance.

CHAPTER 8: UNFOLDING ALLIANCE

Russia-China Dynamics

Russia and China, often perceived as close allies, have been showing signs of a strengthening bond especially in the backdrop of Russia's ongoing conflict in Ukraine. However, this alliance might have deeper implications, transcending mere camaraderie and hinting at a strategic realignment in global politics.

Just before the Russian invasion of Ukraine, leaders of Russia and China, Putin and Xi, held a meeting, declaring their partnership as limitless. This was a strong message to the world, showcasing a united front against any adversarial dynamics, especially from the West.

Since the conflict began, China has avoided condemning Russia's actions in Ukraine. This was evident in various international forums, most notably at the United Nations, where China abstained from voting against Russia's annexation of parts of Ukraine. This abstention speaks volumes about China's strategic positioning, aligning more with Russia's security concerns regarding NATO's expansion in Eastern Europe, while criticizing the US and NATO for fueling the conflict through arms supplies to Ukraine.

As Russia faced challenges in exporting oil and gas to Europe due to sanctions, China stepped in, increasing its energy purchases from Russia by 60% compared to the previous year. This economic support has provided Russia with essential funds to sustain its military operations in Ukraine, showcasing a tangible dimension of the Russia-China alliance. A notable display of military camaraderie was witnessed when Russian and Chinese air forces conducted joint patrols close to Japanese and South Korea air defense zones, coinciding with President Joe Biden's visit to Asia. This joint military venture sent a clear signal to the West about the evolving alliance between Russia and China.

The synergy between Moscow and Beijing has been developing over the past several years, even before the Ukrainian conflict. This growing alliance appears to be moving towards a more structured form, possibly as a counterbalance to Western influence. The unfolding Russia-China alliance is not just a transient diplomatic camaraderie but seems to be evolving into a strategic partnership with economic, military, and political dimensions. This partnership could potentially reshape the geopolitical landscape, warranting a keen understanding and a thorough examination from global stakeholders to fathom its broader implications.

The Geopolitical Tug of War

The relationship between Russia and China has been strengthening over the years, with a spotlight on military alliance. This collaboration, although making sense in the current geopolitical scenario, may evolve differently in the decades to come. Both nations, with their authoritative regimes, aim to shift the Eurasian status quo in their favor, each having distinct geopolitical goals.

Historically, Russia has always aimed to control a significant portion of the Eurasian steppe, especially in the west. This vast flat plain, starting from Northern Germany and extending eastward into Russia, is crucial for Russia's security. During the

Cold War, through the Warsaw Pact, Russia had an extensive control over this region, reaching all the way to Germany. This geographical control created a sort of buffer, making any potential invasion from the west, like from NATO, difficult.

However, post the Soviet Union's collapse in the 1990s, Russia witnessed a decline in its control over this strategic area. Germany reunified, former Warsaw Pact countries joined NATO, and even the Baltic republics aligned with NATO. However, Belarus remained aligned with Moscow. This alignment shifted the focus to Ukraine, marking a red line for Russia's security strategy in Eastern Europe.

The alliance between Russia and China is viewed as a strategic counter to the western influence, especially with the current dynamics in Eastern Europe. They have shown military camaraderie and economic support to each other. However, this alliance is more of a convenience in the current geopolitical setting, and the longevity of this partnership is questionable as the geopolitical landscape evolves.

While the current alliance between Russia and China serves their interests, the future may present different challenges and opportunities. The evolution of this alliance will largely depend on how the geopolitical and economic scenarios unfold in Eurasia and globally. The Sino-Russian alliance is a critical aspect of the modern geopolitical landscape. However, with changing global dynamics and individual national interests, the future of this alliance remains uncertain. Understanding the geopolitical goals of both Russia and China, and the implications of their alliance, is crucial for gauging the future political and military landscape of Eurasia.

Defense Moves on the Chessboard

Russia's strategic moves in Eastern Europe reveal a pattern of safeguarding its territorial integrity. The focal point of its apprehensions lies in Ukraine and Georgia, regions significant for Russia's military and geopolitical security. By analyzing Russia's interventions in these areas, we can comprehend its larger defensive strategy against potential threats from NATO and the U.S.

Russia has always been wary of Western military alliances encroaching on its borders. The alliance of various Eastern European countries with NATO heightened Russia's concerns. Especially troubling for Russia was the potential NATO membership of Ukraine and Georgia, which would bring a hostile military presence dangerously close to key Russian territories. Russia's intervention in Georgia in 2008 was a clear move to establish a buffer zone. By occupying about 20% of Georgia's territory, including Abkhazia, Russia effectively blocked the western coastal entrance to the Eurasian steppe, keeping NATO at arm's length.

Ukraine's potential alignment with NATO was a red flag for Russia. If Ukraine joined NATO, it would allow NATO forces a direct path into the heart of Russia through a vast stretch of flat terrain. This prompted Russia to act in 2014, annexing Crimea to block the Black Sea entrance to the Eurasian steppe and to deter Ukraine from moving closer to NATO.

Chechnya's Significance

Across the Greater Caucasus Mountains lies Chechnya, a region that has historically sought independence from Russia. Despite Russia quelling the rebellions in the 1990s, the idea of a hostile military alliance stationed near Chechnya remains a serious concern for Moscow.

Russia's actions in Ukraine and Georgia unveil a defensive strategy aimed at countering perceived threats from the west. By controlling key geographic points, Russia aims to create buffer zones that would complicate any potential military advances from NATO. The chessboard of Eastern Europe continues to reflect the intricate play of geopolitics, with each move carrying ramifications not just for Russia, but for the broader region and its alliance dynamics.

CHAPTER 9: THE EASTERN CONCERN

China's Geopolitical Chessboard

While Russia engages in territorial defense in Eastern Europe, China, on the other side of Eurasia, faces its own geopolitical challenges. The key to understanding China's actions is identifying its main objectives and the perceived threats from the U.S and its allies.

China's Prime Objectives

1. Reunification with Taiwan

- China aims to bring Taiwan under its control, ending the Chinese Civil War saga. Whether through dialogue or force, this goal remains a priority.

2. Securing Energy Supplies

- To sustain its booming industrial economy, China needs a steady flow of energy resources. Ensuring these channels remain open is vital.

Perceived Encirclement by the U.S and Allies

The U.S, although not a formal ally, supports Taiwan militarily. China fears that any aggressive move towards Taiwan could trigger a U.S-led intervention. The U.S has fostered alliances with Japan, South Korea, the Philippines, and others, forming a network of partnerships that China views as an encirclement. This network, including the Quad (comprising the U.S, India, Japan, and Australia), aims at counterbalancing China's rise. The alliances have effectively confined China's naval capabilities to its immediate coastlines. This limitation hampers China's power projection and control over crucial maritime trade routes.

China's Perception of Containment

China feels cornered by the U.S and its allies in the Indo-Pacific region. The alliances and partnerships formed against it, in its view, threaten its national objectives and regional influence. The scenario echoes the situation in Eastern Europe, where Russia faces encirclement by NATO. The parallel narratives of Russia and China highlight the complex geopolitical chessboard of Eurasia. As both nations pursue their interests, the U.S and its allies' actions in these regions contribute to the escalating tensions. The interactions among these powers, driven by historical grievances and future aspirations, shape the dynamics of global geopolitics.

The Maritime Chessboard: China's Geostrategic Tussle

China's geopolitical ambitions are not confined to land; a significant part of its strategic calculus plays out in the nearby seas. It's a game of maritime chess where control over crucial waterways and islands could determine the nation's security and influence in the broader region.

China views Taiwan as a part of its territory, considering it a rebellious province under the Republic of China (ROC), which fled there post Chinese Civil War. This war never officially concluded, leaving a legacy of discord. Taking over Taiwan is a prime objective. However, China fears the U.S. Navy could disrupt its maritime energy supplies during a conflict over Taiwan, particularly through the vital Strait of Malacca.

Strategic Waterways

1. Strait of Malacca Dilemma

- Over 70% of China's oil and liquefied natural gas imports traverse through the narrow Strait of Malacca. A U.S. blockade here during a conflict could severely hamper China's economy and military operations.

2. South China Sea Claims

- China claims a large part of the South China Sea, marked by the "nine-dash line," extending almost to the Strait of Malacca. This claim, based on historical assertions rather than legal grounds, puts China at odds with many neighboring countries.

Airspace and Island Disputes

1. East China Sea Airspace

- China's declared air defense zone in the East China Sea overlaps with those of Japan, South Korea, and Taiwan, leading to territorial disputes in the skies.

2. Island Controversies

- Beyond the seas, a set of islands administered by Japan are also claimed by China, adding another layer of contention.

China's assertive claims and the perceived encirclement by U.S.-friendly regimes amplify the geopolitical tension in the region. These maritime and territorial disputes reflect the larger contest of power and influence in the Indo-Pacific, with the U.S. and China at the center of this evolving drama. The maritime chessboard is a complex arena where China's aspirations, regional disputes, and the broader U.S.-China rivalry converge. The moves made by each player in this arena will significantly impact the security and geopolitical landscape of the region, echoing far beyond the waters of the East and South China Seas.

CHAPTER 10: A SYMBIOTIC TIE

The Russia-China Resource Balance

In the unfolding geopolitical drama, Russia and China find themselves pitted against the US and its allies. However, aside from political alignments, a deeper layer of symbiosis is at play between Russia and China, based on the complementary nature of their economic strengths and weaknesses.

The Resource Dilemma

1. China's Resource Hunger

- With a booming population and a thriving industrial base, China's demand for natural resources is soaring. However, the nation falls short in domestic supplies, especially in oil, gas, and essential minerals. This shortfall forces China to look abroad for securing these crucial resources.

2. Russia's Resource Abundance

- On the flip side, Russia is a treasure trove of natural resources. It boasts of being one of the leading global reserves of natural gas, oil, coal, and various valuable minerals. However, Russia's economy is much smaller compared to China, and its capital and manpower are inadequate to fully harness these resource riches.

The Strategic Intersection

1. Filling the Void

- The contrasting economic landscapes of China and Russia

lead to a natural intersection of interests. China's capital and Russia's resources form a symbiotic relation where each fills the void of the other.

2. Proximity Advantage

- Most of Russia's resources are tucked away in its Asian part, particularly Siberia, which is geographically closer to China. This geographical closeness is a strategic advantage that can be leveraged to build a robust supply chain to fuel China's industrial engines.

The Larger Implication

1. A Balancing Act

- With China's financial muscle, Russia can unlock the potential of its far-eastern resource bases, which otherwise remain underutilized due to lack of capital and manpower. On the other hand, Russia's resources can help in reducing China's dependency on far-flung sources, especially those passing through geopolitically sensitive regions like the Strait of Malacca.

2. United Against a Common Perception

- Both nations perceive a common pattern of containment from the US and its allies, which adds a geopolitical layer to their economic cooperation. This mutual interest creates a basis for a stronger alliance, at least in the short to medium term.

The Russia-China resource balance showcases a classic example of how economics and geopolitics are intertwined. The complementing economic interests provide a solid ground for Russia and China to collaborate, despite the broader geopolitical tensions that envelop them. This symbiotic relationship not only addresses their individual economic challenges but also presents a united front in the larger geopolitical chessboard.

The Temporal Nature of the Sino-Russian Alliance

At a glance, the alliance between Russia and China appears to be a strong bond forged to counter the American influence in their respective regions. However, digging deeper into history reveals that this alliance may be more of a convenience than a long-term partnership.

Historical Conflicts:

1. Russia's Eastern Foes

- Russia has faced adversaries from the East dating back to the 13th-century Mongol conquest. More recent conflicts include skirmishes with Japan in the early 20th century.

2. China's Century of Humiliation

- Between 1839 and 1949, China experienced what it refers to as a "Century of Humiliation," falling prey to European powers and losing significant territories like Hong Kong and Taiwan.

Temporary Alliance

1. Current Geopolitical Advantages

- At present, China and Russia find themselves against common perceived adversaries, primarily the US. Their cooperation helps China secure essential resources from Russia, while Russia gains the capital necessary to counter American influence in Eastern Europe.

2. Strategic Depth and Resource Security

- Through this alliance, Russia aims to expand its strategic depth across the Eurasian steppe, while China seeks to reduce its resource dependency on volatile maritime routes, particularly through the Strait of Malacca.

Future Implications

1. Historical Rivalries

- Historically, China and Russia are more accustomed to rivalry rather than friendship. The current alliance is a deviation from a long history of competition and conflict.

2. Territorial Resentments

- Despite the end of China's Century of Humiliation with the establishment of the People's Republic in 1949, some territorial grievances remain. Taiwan, once seized by Japan, remains outside Beijing's control. Similarly, Hong Kong remained under British rule until 1997, reflecting the lasting impact of historical territorial concessions.

The Sino-Russian alliance stands on a complex historical and geopolitical foundation. While their collaboration serves their short-term interests well, historical rivalries and territorial resentments lurk beneath the surface. As the geopolitical landscape evolves, the durability and longevity of this alliance may be tested, possibly reverting the relationship back to its historical norm of rivalry rather than cooperation.

CHAPTER 11: THE IRONY OF HISTORY AND THE SINO-RUSSIAN DYNAMICS

The modern alliance between China and Russia comes with a deep undertone of historical irony. The land that now holds significant strategic military bases for Russia was once forcefully taken from China, a dark episode that still lingers in the memory of Chinese nationalists.

1. The Seizure of Outer Manchuria

- In 1858, during a time of turmoil within China due to internal civil war and external conflicts like the Second Opium War, Russia capitalized on China's vulnerability. With a show of military force at the border, they coerced the Qing dynasty into signing over a vast territory known as Outer Manchuria.

2. The Unequal Treaty of 1860

- Under the pressure of Russian troops and not wanting to engage in another war, the Qing dynasty signed a treaty in 1860, relinquishing a large tract of land equivalent to the size of Ukraine to Russia without a single shot fired. This treaty is seen as one of the many unequal treaties China was forced into during its Century of Humiliation.

Strategic Importance

1. Formation of Key Russian Cities

- This acquired land later proved to be immensely beneficial for Russia, as it founded significant cities like Khabarovsk and Vladivostok in what used to be Outer Manchuria. Vladivostok became Russia's largest Pacific port, housing its Pacific Fleet including nuclear-armed submarines, a critical part of Russia's naval strategy.

2. China's Loss

- The treaty locked China away from direct access to the Sea of Japan, confining them to the East and South China Seas. This geographical limitation altered China's naval and trade dynamics considerably.

Resentment and Remembrance

1. Never Forgotten

- The loss of Outer Manchuria is a painful memory for many Chinese nationalists, including notable figures like Mao Zedong, the founder of the People's Republic of China. This loss is grouped with other unequal treaties that China was forced into, a stark reminder of its past humiliations.

2. Sino-Soviet Split

- Relations between China and the Soviet Union soured significantly in the 1960s due to ideological differences and territorial disputes, among other factors. The bitterness from the past played a part in the discord between these two neighbors.

The alliance between China and Russia today is a strategic one, overshadowed by a history of exploitation and territorial aggression. As these two nations navigate their modern alliance, the bitter memories of the past remain a silent narrative in their complex relationship, hinting at an undercurrent of historical grievance amidst present-day cooperation.

The Sino-Soviet Border Conflict: An Echo of Past Grievances

Amidst a turbulent global stage, a historical grievance resurfaced between China and the Soviet Union in the 1960s, leading to a dangerous military confrontation. The disagreement was rooted in their differing claims over border territories, a reminder of the past annexation of Outer Manchuria by Russia.

Ideological Disagreement

1. Marxism-Leninism Rift

- The relationship between China and the Soviet Union began to fray due to their different interpretations of Marxism-Leninism. This ideological discord was more than just a theoretical disagreement; it represented a deeper rivalry and distrust between the two communist giants.

2. Mao's Resentment

- Mao Zedong, the leader of China, privately voiced his discontent about Russia's unilateral annexation of Outer Manchuria. His comments, though initially private, were leaked, inciting outrage in Moscow.

The Brezhnev Doctrine

1. Soviet Interventionism

- In 1968, following the invasion of Czechoslovakia to quash a revolt, the Soviet Union under Brezhnev announced a doctrine that granted them the right to intervene in any communist country straying from the global communist movement as defined by Moscow. This doctrine alarmed Mao, who saw it as a potential threat to his rule and China's autonomy.

Border Dispute Ignites

1. Disputed Territory

- The Sino-Soviet border in the Far East was marked by the Amur and Ussuri rivers. While the Soviets claimed the borders were at the river banks on the Chinese side, China argued that the border ran through the middle of the rivers, making the islands on their side of the line Chinese territory.

2. Flashpoint on the River

- The disagreement escalated in March 1969 over an island known as Shenbao to the Chinese and Damansky to the Soviets. What followed was a fierce battle, with hundreds of troops clashing and casualties on both sides. This island dispute was more than a minor skirmish; it was a symbol of unresolved historical grievances and escalating tensions between two nuclear-armed neighbors.

Brink of a Larger Conflict

1. Tensions Escalate

- The conflict had the potential to spiral into a full-blown war. With over ten thousand rounds of artillery exchanged and the looming threat of nuclear engagement, the stakes were perilously high.

2. Soviet Fears

- Soviet commanders were reportedly terrified of a greater war with China. The disparity in troop numbers near the border, with China having over one and a half million soldiers compared to the Soviet's 350,000, was a stark reminder of the volatile situation.

The Sino-Soviet border conflict was a manifestation of historical grievances, ideological discord, and territorial ambitions. As the dust settled, the reverberations of this confrontation echoed through the annals of history, leaving a legacy of distrust and rivalry that overshadowed Sino-Soviet relations for decades to come.

CHAPTER 12: UNRESOLVED GRIEVANCES

Shifting Allegiances in Central Asia

The uneasy calm following the Sino-Soviet border skirmishes of 1969 did little to erase historical grievances. While the border was eventually agreed upon in 1991, the actions of Russia in Ukraine years later rekindled fears of potential territorial ambitions, echoing past grievances of unfair treaties and annexations. Meanwhile, a new arena of competition emerges as China and Russia vie for influence in the resource-rich, strategically positioned Central Asia.

Historical Grievances: The Ghost of Outer Manchuria

The Soviet Union, outnumbered in troops along the border, harbored fears that Mao's China might attempt to reclaim Outer Manchuria, a historical wound dating back to 1860. The extreme option of using nuclear weapons to deter a vastly superior Chinese force was a chilling reminder of the stakes involved. The border was officially settled in 1991, but Russia's actions in Ukraine, reneging on treaties and annexing territories based on historical claims, opened a Pandora's box. The fear lurked that China might one day pursue its historical claim to Outer Manchuria, reigniting old wounds.

Central Asia: The New Frontier

Post the Soviet Union collapse, five new countries emerged in Central Asia. Over the decades, these nations have gradually drifted from Russia's orbit, inching closer to China. China's ambitious Belt and Road Initiative aims to resurrect the ancient Silk Road trade routes traversing Central Asia. This initiative not only promises economic boons but also significantly elevates China's influence in the region, potentially at Russia's expense. As China makes inroads into Central Asia, the competition with Russia intensifies. The region, rich in natural resources and offering a vital geostrategic position, becomes a chessboard where the two giants maneuver for influence. Russia faces a dilemma as its traditional sphere of influence is encroached upon. The situation begs the question of how Russia will respond to maintain its foothold in the region against China's economic onslaught.

Central Asia - A Stage for New Engagements

The quest for resources and influence directs China's lens towards Central Asia, a region historically under Russian sway. As China endeavors to revive ancient trade routes, Russia grapples with waning influence amidst China's economic allure. Yet, a common objective surfaces: stability, especially in the backdrop of China's internal discord in Xinjiang.

Central Asia, rich in oil and gas, beckons China as it seeks to satiate its growing energy hunger. Through the Belt and Road Initiative, China establishes pipelines from resource-abundant nations like Turkmenistan, Uzbekistan, and Kazakhstan. This endeavor significantly cuts down China's reliance on sea-based gas imports traversing the risky Malacca Strait.

The economic dividends of China's engagement are palpable. China now stands as a principal trade partner to these Central Asian nations, overshadowing Russia. The shift in trade dynamics provides these nations an alternative to Russia's economic embrace.

Russia's aspiration to keep Central Asia within its economic ambit through the Eurasian Economic Union faces a setback as three nations lean towards China's Belt and Road Initiative. The shift underscores a dwindling Russian influence in its traditional backyard. Central Asia holds geostrategic importance to Russia as a buffer against historical invasion routes into the Eurasian steppe. Yet, the growing Chinese footprint necessitates a delicate balancing act for Russia to maintain its strategic interests while acknowledging China's rising influence.

China's Dual Objective

Beyond resource acquisition, China eyes Central Asia as a linchpin to stabilize its restive Xinjiang province. The region, marred by ethnic and religious discord, poses a significant internal security challenge to China. By the early 2010s, the turbulence in Xinjiang escalated, prompting a severe crackdown by the Chinese government around 2012. Border security tightens as China's armed forces bolster their presence to quell unrest and ensure stability.

Central Asia emerges as a canvas where Sino-Russian interactions paint a complex picture. While economic and geostrategic interests drive China's deepening engagement, Russia navigates a tightrope of historical influence and present-day realities. Amidst this, the quest for stability in Xinjiang adds another layer to China's objectives in the region, intertwining internal security with broader geopolitical maneuvers.

CHAPTER 13: THE BREWING WATER CRISIS

China faces a water crisis, a problem exacerbated by an unequal distribution of water resources within its territory. The north, housing major cities and a significant chunk of the population, is particularly parched. As climate change intensifies, the crisis deepens, bringing a new layer of complexity to the Sino-Russian dynamics.

Discrepancy in Water Distribution

China shelters about 20% of the global population but holds merely 7% of the world's fresh surface water. The disparity becomes glaring in the North China Plain, where major cities like Beijing and Tianjin reside. Despite being home to over 400 million people, the region's local water resources are comparable to those in arid Saudi Arabia. A significant portion (80%) of China's water resources is nestled in the southern part and Tibet, creating a stark regional imbalance. To bridge the gap, water from these regions is transported to the north through pipes and aqueducts.

Climate Change - A Harsh Reality

Climate change is not a distant threat but a harsh reality for China. In 2022, a severe drought further strained the already scarce water resources, painting a grim picture of the future. The drought amplifies China's quest for water security, which may require looking beyond its borders. This quest could potentially direct China's eyes towards neighboring Russia, a nation abundant in fresh water resources.

Water could emerge as a new point of engagement between China and Russia. While Russia has ample water resources, China's growing desperation for water might drive negotiations or arrangements. Russia, on the one hand, needs to maintain its strategic focus on the west; on the other, it can't overlook the potential leverage its water resources provide against a thirsty neighbor.

Water scarcity in China unveils a potential arena of Sino-Russian interaction. The unfolding water crisis, intertwined with climate change, could either forge new collaborations or breed contention between these two powerful neighbors. As the taps run dry in the north, China's approach towards ensuring water security could significantly impact its relations with Russia, adding a new dimension to the geopolitics of the region.

The Undercurrents of Water Diplomacy

The specter of water scarcity is casting a long shadow over China, especially after the 2022 severe drought. With neighboring countries like India also grappling with water issues, China's gaze might shift northward towards Russia's abundant freshwater resources, particularly Lake Baikal. This chapter delves into the dynamics surrounding China's interest in this massive freshwater reservoir and the potential ramifications on Sino-Russian relations.

Lake Baikal - A Liquid Treasure

Lake Baikal, situated very close to China's borders, is the largest freshwater lake by volume, holding more water than all of North America's Great Lakes combined. It's a colossal reservoir that could cater to the global population's drinking needs for around 50 years. Chinese interest in this liquid treasure manifested in the 2010s when a state-owned company, AquaSib, started acquiring land around Lake Baikal. In 2017, the firm unveiled plans to build a pipeline to transport water to China, revealing a glimpse of China's potential strategy to address its water scarcity.

The Backlash and Beyond

The pipeline proposal ignited a wave of protests among the local Russian populace. They feared that such a venture might deplete or harm their precious water resource, showcasing the inherent tension in sharing transboundary water resources. The pipeline proposal not only highlighted local concerns but also hinted at a potential diplomatic dilemma. If pursued further, water might become a new axis of negotiation or contention between China and Russia, adding another layer of complexity to their multifaceted relationship. China's growing thirst may drive it to explore agreements with Russia regarding Lake Baikal's water. However, such discussions could be delicate, balancing the desperate need for water with the geopolitical realities and the local sentiments in Russia.

Water scarcity is a ticking time bomb not just for China, but for many parts of the world. However, the quest for water security could open new diplomatic channels or trigger disputes, especially when it involves shared or neighboring resources like Lake Baikal. As China mulls over solutions to its water crisis, the Baikal equation with Russia is bound to be a part of a larger geopolitical calculus. How these two giants navigate the waters of diplomacy amid the undercurrents of local and global challenges will be a narrative worth following in the coming years.

CHAPTER 14: SHIFTING BALANCES IN THE FAR EAST

The geopolitics between Russia and China are becoming increasingly intertwined as they navigate their interests in the resource-rich, yet sparsely populated Russian Far East. This chapter discusses the evolving dynamics, the demographic and economic contrasts, and the potential implications on their positions on the world stage.

Demographic and Economic Disparities

The Russian Far East, despite its vast resources, is home to only 8 million Russians, with half residing in the former China-controlled Outer Manchuria. In contrast, over 109 million Chinese live in the three provinces bordering the Far East. The stark 13 to 1 population ratio emphasizes the demographic disparity between the two regions. With China's economy roaring, its need for resources like water, oil, gas, and coal is escalating. The proximity and resource abundance of the Russian Far East make it a focal point for China's resource acquisition efforts.

Russian Far East's Population Decline

The Russian Far East witnessed a population decline of over 100,000 people between 2012 and 2018, a trend exacerbated by the Covid-19 pandemic and the conflict in Ukraine. These events have further isolated Russia, restricting access to Western capital. Faced with a dwindling population and economic constraints, Russia is gradually opening up the Far East to Chinese investment and labor. Although this has been a point of resistance due to fears of demographic domination by the numerically superior Chinese, the circumstances are driving Russia towards this inevitable cooperation.

Tilting Scales of Power

The increasing dependence on Chinese capital and labor for developing the Russian Far East's resources hints at a shifting power balance. As Russia leans more towards China for economic sustenance, it edges closer to becoming a junior partner in this geopolitical duo. The evolving dynamics are unlikely to escape Beijing's notice. The shift towards a more China-centric alliance could significantly impact the broader Sino-Russian relations and their joint stance on global issues.

The Russian Far East's demographic and economic scenario is painting a new picture in the Sino-Russian narrative. As Russia leans on Chinese investment to fuel its Far East's development, the balance of power subtly tilts, crafting a pathway where China might hold more cards in the partnership. The unfolding dynamics in this region are a microcosm of the broader geopolitical ballet, with each move choreographed by the pressing needs of survival, growth, and influence.

CHAPTER 15: THE FRAGILE BALANCE OF SINO-RUSSIAN RELATIONS

As Russia leans towards China for economic sustenance due to its strained relations with Europe, the dynamics of their alliance could shift significantly. Presently, both countries find common ground in opposing the United States' influence. This shared goal promotes their alliance as Russia seeks alternative economic partners, and China aims to secure its northern borders while accessing inexpensive resources overland, reducing its dependence on maritime energy imports through the Malacca Strait. Russia is currently providing China with significant benefits, like discounted oil and gas supplies and free economic reign in Central Asia, which aids China in distracting the United States from the Indo-Pacific region.

The Uncertain Horizon

The partnership's stability may be tested if there's a change in Russia's political landscape. Should a less China-friendly government come to power, the alliance could face challenges. China has often cited historical claims to justify its territorial ambitions. If Beijing becomes the dominant partner, there's a concern that it might assert historical claims over parts of Russia's Far East, especially if there's a dispute over resource pricing or supply.

Potential Future Scenarios

If the common adversarial stance against the US persists, the Sino-Russian alliance may continue to thrive, with China benefiting from discounted resources and Russia from economic cooperation. Alternatively, a change in leadership or disagreements over resource allocations might strain relations. If Russia attempts to renegotiate terms, or if China asserts territorial claims, tensions could escalate. With a stronger economic position, China might dictate the terms of the alliance, possibly leveraging its historical claims to assert more control, especially if Russia becomes more desperate.

The Sino-Russian alliance stands at a crossroads shaped by geopolitical, economic, and historical factors. The interplay of leadership, economic dependency, and historical claims will significantly impact the future course of their relations. While a common adversary keeps them aligned for now, the underlying disparities and historical grievances hint at a fragile alliance, susceptible to future geopolitical shifts.

EPILOGUE

*Sino-Russian Dynamics: An
Odyssey of Power Balance*

The enthralling journey through the labyrinth of Sino-Russian relations unveils an intricate mosaic of power play, historical grievances, and strategic maneuvering. As the world pivots into a new era, the alliance between these two behemoths is more than a mere coincidence of interests; it's a testament to the realpolitik that continues to shape the global order. This tale of camaraderie and competition is painted on a broad canvas of historical legacy, geopolitical imperatives, and an unyielding quest for regional and global ascendancy.

1. Historical Resonance

The echoes of the past reverberate through the annals of Sino-Russian relations. The saga of Outer Manchuria, the wounds of historical conflicts, and the shadows of ideological discord delineate a relationship fraught with both synergy and suspicion.

2. Resource Quest

The relentless pursuit of resources has been a recurring theme in this narrative. From the energy corridors of Central Asia to the freshwater jewels of Siberia, the quest for resource security unveils a dynamic of mutual dependence and rivalry.

3. Geopolitical Choreography

The choreography on the geopolitical stage reflects a delicate dance between cooperation and competition. Whether in the steppes of Central Asia or the turbulent waters of the South China Sea, the Sino-Russian duet plays out against a backdrop of shifting power dynamics.

4. The Ukrainian Interlude

The unfolding drama in Ukraine serves as a poignant subplot in this narrative, highlighting the fluidity of international alliances and the potential for external events to reshape the Sino-Russian dynamics.

5. Future Trajectories

As the curtains draw on this chapter of global geopolitics, the path ahead remains shrouded in uncertainty. The entente may endure, fueled by a shared desire to counterbalance western hegemony, or fissures may emerge, propelled by historical grievances and competing interests.

6. The Global Reverb

The resonance of Sino-Russian relations is felt far beyond their borders. It's a narrative that entwines with the destinies of nations near and far, underscoring the indelible imprint of this alliance on the world stage.

7. A Call for Astute Navigation

As the globe spins into uncharted territories, astute navigation through the complex Sino-Russian dynamics is paramount for global stability. Understanding the nuances of this relationship is not merely an academic endeavor but a requisite for prudent policy formulation and strategic foresight.

In encapsulation, the Sino-Russian narrative is a riveting

expedition through the meandering rivers of geopolitics, with currents that shape, and are shaped by, the broader global milieu. The depth of historical engagements, the breadth of their strategic interests, and the spectrum of possible future interactions offer a rich tapestry for contemplation and analysis. Through the lens of Sino-Russian dynamics, we glean insights into the enduring essence of geopolitics, the perennial quest for power, and the profound impact of historical legacies on contemporary global relations.